Old Wine

the *Poetry* of

Dr. John R. Strum

inner child press, ltd.

General Information

Old Wine

Dr. John R. Strum

1st Edition : 2012

Publisher Information

1st Edition : Inner Child Press
innerchildpress@gmail.com
www.innerchildpress.com

This Collection is protected under U.S. and International Copyright Laws

Copyright © 2012 : Dr. John R. Strum
LOC : 1-772465447

ISBN-13 : 978-0615649528
ISBN-10 : 0615649521

Cover Design :   William S. Peters, Sr.
Edited by :   Janet P. Caldwell

$ 16.95

*D*edication

to my Wife

Robyn Lorraine Strum

my Sister

Sue Goldzweig

...both of whom have been so important in my life.

*F*oreword

There is a song lyric that says, "Dance like nobody's watching," and John R. Strum's poetry certainly does that. Whether the music speaks of love, joy, satanic musings, or a dream of death, Strum's poetry invites the reader to join in no matter what music is playing or who is playing it:

> *I cannot believe,* he tells us,
> *That our God*
> *Is the ultimate creator.*

Once into these dances, we see that our view is not front and center, rather it is the view from behind a curtain, through the keyhole or through binoculars from some mountain peak far away. Readers are invited to see/hear what goes on in John Strum's poems, but he reminds them that there are mysteries:

> *What do you know about me?*
> *Can you read my thoughts?*
> *...Where is the wisdom*
> *So proudly proclaimed by my colouring?*

A retired forensic psychiatrist, he now spends most of his time writing. His great love is poetry. John R. Strum has obviously gained a respect for what humankind might come down to in the end. He makes his own inquiries, hopes readers will self-examine, and then reminds them that, even those inquiries and examinations may not net them all they'd like to know :

> *I am not one*
> he says
> *I am a multitude,*
> *Living a multitude of lives*
> *In preparation*
> *For what is to come.*

In "Wizard of Oz," Strum speaks of the "ultimate shaman." Perhaps he is speaking about himself—his own ability to "engage the power of dreams." However he sees himself, John R. Strum's invitation to the dance is a clear one. Don't sit this one out.

Martina Reisz Newberry
Palm Springs, CA 2012

Preface

Although this collection contains some of my earlier work going back to the turn of the century, most is recent, since my retirement.

Essentially it is a collection devoted to the later years of life. It is about all aspects of life: past, present and future, real and imagined. It deals with emotions and ruminations also some real, some imagined. I have tried to inject humour and I have tried to present alternative points of view..

One of my aims has been to show that artistic endeavour such as writing poetry does not necessarily deteriorate with increasing years and that is possible to have a perspective which is different to the one which one may have had in earlier times.

I have tried not to endorse causes and to give respect to a variety of points of view.

I hope that it will give as much pleasure to the reader as it has given to the writer.

Bob Strum

Table of Contents

Table of Contents . . . continued

Table of Contents . . . continued

Table of Contents . . . continued

If I am not for myself, who will be for me ?

And when I am for myself, what am 'I' ?

And If not now, when?

Hillel the Elder

Dr. John R. Strum

Old Wine

the *Poetry* of

Dr. John R. Strum

inner child press, ltd.

Abyssinian Seduction

Little squeak, little squeak

Don't let all the people peak

Running, running down the hall

Backward glance, a lover's call.

Into bed, a mighty leap

Not for you a wish to sleep.

Licking fingers, licking toes

Biting ears and biting nose.

Rolling, wriggling on your back

Never frightened to attack

Tummy rubbed, oh! what delight

Off again, the world's all right.

Thank you Tess for what you do

No surprise I love you too!

A Time To Reflect

Last Friday I turned seventy five
And it occurs to me
How strange it is that I survive.
I wonder why I am alive
Whilst other souls roam free.

I feel the slowing of my mind.
My memory betrays
A drift away from humankind.
I fear I will be left behind,
The ending of my days.

The tides have swept me out to sea.
The shorelines disappear.
The angry waves lash out at me.
False promises to set me free.
I'm overcome with fear.

My prison is a leaky ship.
Its timbers rot away.
The crew has let the lifelines slip.
The sails are rotting too. They rip
All hope from me. I pray.

I pray to saints I have not known
That they may intercede.
I know I can't survive alone.
My past, my sins are all I own.
No hope that I be freed.

There is no way to understand
Our pain. Mankind dismay!
No loving God will hold my hand.
There is no hope. No promised land.
We simply pass away

Dr. John R. Strum

A Room With Frosted Windows

Although I am not
Visually impaired,
I sometimes fail to see
What is in front of me.
I fall and break my bones,
My arms often in plaster.
I have
A diminished sense of smell.
I am tone deaf.
I cannot sing,
But I feel the rhythms
Surrounding me.

Isolated from my world
As I am,
How dare I write poetry!
I read the glorious words
Of the true artists,
There is music,
Which they alone can hear.
They share Nature's secrets,
Whispered into their ears.
They know her flow and rhythms,
The shades and nuances,
Her exquisite beauty.
Her wild moods.
Dare I say it?
She is truly feminine.

I see nothing. I hear nothing.
I envy those who are psychic..
I try but do not have the gift.
I search the skies.
The heavens are alive.
I sense my isolation.
Everything is far away
A part of me cries out,
""Idiot, can't you see,
Out there, far away
A reflection of your soul?"
I Scream at the stars,
Hoping to be recognised,
To be heard.
I look inward
To find meaning to my world.

Thank God for poetry,
My Seeing Eye Dog,
Who lets me wander at large.
I must struggle with that
Which comes so naturally to others.
I seek experience of the world
Whilst locked inside a room
With frosted windows.

A Cottage By The Sea

I rented a cottage
By the sea,
Almost as weather beaten
As I was,
With that old frame.
Weatherboard, unpainted,
Showing the effects
Of climate and sea spray.
It was comfortable.
My furniture,
Suitably aged,
Did not look out of place.
There were two bedrooms,
One for me.
One for my computer.
I had a place to work,
A place into which
My soul could flow,
Seeping under doors,
Creating an atmosphere,
Tangible and real.

I felt at home.
So did my cat and dog.
My music and my television
Were in place.
I confess
I love watching all sports.
I did not crave companionship
My team was in its place.
I could fulfil my destiny.
I did not seek fame.
I hoped to share

My soul,
My vision
Of this strange universe
With aliens,
Sporting unseen antennae,
Who sense my meaning
As they remember home,

I have always written.
Sometimes when depressed,
Sometimes hypomanic,
But other aspects of life
Intruded.
Work, family obligations
Dare I say it? Sloth

Retirement set me free
To follow my destiny
Even if it satisfies only me.
My work had given me
Much joy,
Insights into people,
Each one unique
No two faces the same.
No two stories, the same.
A dazzling ballet.
A Hogarth painting.

'The Scream'
Was also
Prominent.

Of course
I wrote about Nature,
Who was at times
Opposed
To God's apparent plan.
There was more.
Who am I? Where am I going?
Who fashioned the mask
I wear?
What lies beneath,
Waiting to be uncovered?
Love, hate,
Rejection,
The pain of loss.
The soul.
Ideals and frustrations.
Alternative realities
Ghosts, from the past,
From the future
And places in between.

This is now my world,
These are my companions.
Unless a Tsunami
Sweeps me away.
Unless my Inner Child
Rebels, declaring,
'Enough is enough.'
I will spend my days here
I feel at home.

A Call To Arms

I listen to the words you say.
You tell me you must go away,
A call to arms. I never knew
My arms were not enough for you.

Who will you fight who will you kill?
Is it your duty or a thrill?
Is there a reason you must fight?
How can killing ever be right?

Go if you must, nothing I say
Will change your mind You'll have your way
Till you return I will be brave.
You think there is a world to save.

And yet I know the crippling pain
I'll feel til you are home again.
I will shed tears and I will grieve
I do not want to let you leave.

Alexander Nevsky

Fantasies can emanate

From within,

Or can be stirred

By the work of others.

Alexander Nevsky was a film,

An Eisenstein masterpiece.

I recall one sequence

Which has stayed with me forever.

I am not sure if my memory was accurate.

Alexander Nevsky Continued

Two armies. armour, horses
On each side of a frozen lake.
All kneeling,
Whilst their bishops blessed them.
Each army reassured
God was on their side.
They could not loose the day.

They put on armour.
They mounted.
They charged,
Meeting in the centre of the lake
The ice collapsed.
Both armies disappeared,
Drowned by the icy waters.
Not every soldier
Wanted to be there,
But they knew
Deserters, stragglers
Would be killed.

There was a line
Of frightened prisoners
In concentration camp
Being herded in a line
To the gas chamber.
They moved forward
Prodded by bayonets.
Stragglers,
Those taking flight
Instantly shot.

Humanity
Is constantly
Prodded forwards
They have but one
Destination
Death.

Fodder for the meek
Who apparently
Shall inherit the earth.

Bacteria, viruses
Even cancer cells
Feed on those
Who have escaped
Other forms of death

It seems
That living flesh
Is not important.
It is only the packaging
For precious contents .
Released,
To continue their journey
To a rendezvous
With God.

AIDS

Aids will never weary them,
Yet the churches all condemn.
Death will be their final rest.
Medication failed the test.
Millions die the world just shrugs.
Some risked sex and some took drugs.

Blood transfusion snatched a few.
No one knew what they should do.
Some went on a sexual spree,
Spreading death with evil glee.
Once more, nature did contrive
Cutting numbers left alive.

Plague and famine ,sometimes war,
Signs that we could not ignore.
Do we really understand
Nature when she takes a hand?
Only one thing does make sense,
Human insignificance.

Value days which still remain.
Conquering your fears and pain.
Links you formed through family,
Joy you spread so liberally,
Form the ties that just might save
Parts of you beyond the grave.

Autumn

In the autumn of my life
The days were disappearing.
Time accelerating,
There were beautiful young people
Bursting with vitality and hope,
Bound upon wondrous journeys.
Which I would never make.
I felt the early frosts of winter
caressing my body, licking my cheeks
An unwanted lover intent on rape.
There was little comfort to be found
In waning fires.
The Summer sun, hot and seductive
Had stirred my soul in bygone years
Flames of passion, consumed my life..
I would follow with lascivious eyes
the seductive walk of countless temptresses.
Sometimes our souls would touch.
We would join in timeless dance,
Singing the songs of nature
In perfect harmony.

Burning Driftwood

A moonlit night
The silken sands, which separate
The bushland from the restless sea.
Two lovers come to consummate
Their passions. Innocent and free
From all constraints of wrong and right.

We were fifteen,
Lost in the magic of the night.
Quite innocent of guilt or shame.
Ecstatic in our shared delight
And burning driftwood, gentle flame
Had cast its spell upon the scene.

I recollect
Two sweet young breasts, delightful lips,
A mossy pillow which demands
Some comfort from my fingertips.
My flesh caressed by tender hands.
We did not know what to expect.

Years come and go.
Where are you now? Perhaps we met,
Passing each other in the street.
Surely we'd know each other, yet
Our aging bodies might defeat
Our glance and we would never know..

Old age conspires
To rob us of our youthful charm.
So little time. The sun will set
My memories, I must keep calm.
Live on and I cannot forget
The burning flames of youthful fires.

Bipolar Bears

You're in for a rocky ride my child,
You who lives inside me
Pretending you are so close to God.
My moods tumble.
After periods of despair
I rise like a clown
In a balloon,
Amusing yet terrifying
The watching crowd,
,Fascinated by my
Gaudy pantaloons,
Fearful of my fall to earth.
No purpose served.
I stagger from situation to situation,
Never in control,
Believing in the certainty
Of immanent disaster,
But also seeing
The goldmines in the sky.
How can anybody believe me?
Why am I not surprised
That few have faith in me?

It's always somebody else's fault.
I am not depressed.
Others have depressed me.
I can turn my inner rage
Against an outer foe.
Rage and despair
Alternating within me.

The grandiosity
Also leads to anger.
Why can't they see
My brilliance?
Is it a conspiracy?
With much difficulty
Frustrated parents or a spouse
Take me to a clinic.
They must think
That I a mad.
The drugs they give me
When I feel so good
Rob me of my, creativity
The other ones
I take only if I can't avoid it
Remove my capacity
To feel.

I am not permitted
To live my life
In my own way.
My independence
Is amputated.
My spirit is drained away.
They used leeches
To drain away bad blood.
What hidden leeches
Drain away my soul?

It is an endless circle.
My moods cause rejection.
Rejection brings on
My moods.
They swing
Like an ocean in a storm.
How will it end?
When will it end?
How can I find tranquilly?
How can I rest?
I have seen tornadoes,
Hurricanes
Uprooting trees,
Blowing cars into the sea,
Causing people to fear,
To flee.
My storm is within.
The havoc and destruction
Are the same.

Are all people
Really created equal?
I think not.
Soldiers go to war.
They fight battles.
Winners or losers,
They return home
If they are still alive.
What battles can I win?
What home would
Welcome my return?

Batyah

I thought I knew you well.
But it was merely an illusion.
You had your life and occupation.
Involved with other people's dreams.
You sang songs of nature, and of love.
I did not know that you were but a shadow of your mother,
Holding her hand, bedazzled by her magic.

You had been a passenger aboard a ship
Bound upon a unique voyage,
Charting your own destiny.
And then she died, and in quiet desperation
You fled your ship to be with her.
Like Lot, like Orpheus,
There was no triumph over death.
The bonds, which tied you to the ship
Dissolved and you were cast adrift,
Floating in an ether of silent detachment

And there you found her,
Transformed into a star, somewhere in the heavens,
Drawing you into her orbit. Trapped.
Destined to travel forever about her essence,
Nurtured only by ancient beliefs
Which had no meaning in your other life.

I see your shadow.
I mourn the passing of the life I knew.
You are transformed forever.
The very bonds, which hold you,
Stop you from reaching her.
There is no future, no past,
Only your loneliness as you cry out her name.

Black Cockatoos

My house has been invaded.
Ants parade in single file
Down my kitchen wall.
Outside, the shrill cry of cockatoos,
Black, raucous,
In the trees, on the lawn.
I look into the sky.
The clouds are gathering
And so, once again
Nature warns of her intent.
Rain!
Later that day
I saunter to my bedroom.
The Bed is so inviting,
But, sadly I return
To my dreary tasks.
Outside, the rain is pelting down.
Where there was lawn
Lakes are forming.
Ah well, the frogs and ducks
Are having fun.

BRAN NUI DAY

In the evening the waters rippled.
The tree tips chatted in the breeze.
A cloudless sky above.
A feeling of comfort and ease.
A flagon of wine from which we tippled.
I was hoping for love.

WE had lain beside the river all day.
I had brought a blanket and wine.
She provided a meal.
Never our intention to dine.
Far more joyous games for us to play.
Precious moments to steal.

No mater that we came from different creeds.
Her headscarf had been caste aside.
We were prepared for this.
Our passion overcame her pride.
We had a desperate need to meet our needs,
More than a simple kiss.

The next day I arose to read the news.
An honour killing had occurred.
Father, uncle, brother,
Had slaughtered her without a word.
Family honour they could not refuse.
They could do no other.

No one even thought to punish me.
A man could not control his lust.
The woman is to blame.
Men do exactly what they must.
And so the man is destined to go free.
She dies to heal the shame.

The authorities said 'what could we expect'.
To act, not politically correct.

Children Of The Holocaust

The weather was far from ideal.
Above her shone a bright full moon.
Not the best evening for escape.
A prison door was left agape.
She only saw one Nazi goon.
The situation seemed unreal.
She walked directly to the man.
Her recitation then began.

She was a girl of fifteen years.
In concentration camps interred.
Her family had all been killed.
She lived because she now was skilled
In sexual games. No guilt incurred.
He soul was dead. She had no fears.
She knew exactly what to say
To help her in her getaway.

"Put down your gun and look on high.
That magic full moon has the power
To make you always think of me.
My face is something you will see
Every day and every hour,
My blood stained corpse will greet your eye.
You will go mad. You cannot hide.
You'll kill your wife and suicide."

The poor wretch dropped his gun and fled
Whilst she walked quickly through the gate.
She was to join a savage crew,
Young girls who knew just what to do.
They'd ride on trains and they would wait
For Nazis who would join the dead.
Murder for them was no big deal
As long as there was cash to steal.

On Berlin streets she plied her trade.
She had the skill to make her way.
She knew that she was on her own.
At end of war she was alone.
But now it was a bright new day.
She'd stolen killed and been a whore.
That part of her life was no more.

She left behind that ravaged land.
Australia would become her home.
Marriage and children filled her life
But she could not forget the strife.
Her ghosts were there at night to roam.
It wasn't hard to understand.
Although, she'd put the past behind,
It haunted her unconscious mind.

I understand the things she did.
That was the way she could survive.
The mental scars had change her soul.
Nothing will fill that gaping hole.
The past would always be alive.
Distortions, which could not be hid.
The evil sadists had their way
She suffered to her dying day.

Candle Light

When I was young
My eyes would
Feast upon
The Sabbath table.
My heart's delight,
The lighting of candles.

I watched my mother
Light the flame.
I rejoiced in the new born life
Which emerged,
As each candle
Was lit.

When I awoke,
I would go to the table
Where the candles
Had lived out
Their brief lives.
I saw a puddle of wax.

I saw the debris
Of moths attracted
To the flame,
The stains
Of candle wax
On the tablecloth.

For now and for the future
I pray.
Let there be light.
Let there be life.

Perhaps the candle's life
Had been more complex
Than I thought.
I look back
Remembering
My enchantment.
I think to myself,
This is our destiny.

Remember me
When you enjoy the flame.
Remember me
When my flame
Has run its course.

Charley

There were pictures in the paper.
Editorials had their say.
Little girl cuddling a teddy
Headline story for the day.

She was lying in an alley.
No one knew how she had died.
Eighteen years! Her life was taken.
What remained was cast aside.

Death deprived her of a mother.
Father was a runaway.
On the streets where she was living
She was just another stray.

I recall an ancient legend.
Hamelin in Germany.
Had a plague of hungry rodents.
Piper paid to make them flee.

City leaders without morals.
Piper selling Mary J.
Children dancing to his music.
Piper took them all away.

Saw a film about a puppet.
Muleteer had promised fun.
Took the kids to Pleasure Island.
Changed to donkeys everyone.

Dr. John R. Strum

We have given up our children
To the streets, to drugs and shame
We have taken it for granted.
No one will accept the blame.

We are told by all the preachers
Love for all, not just the chaste.
How can we believe the message
In the midst of so much waste.

Rest in peace poor little lady
Buried with your teddy bears
Customers will not disturb you
What a shame that no one cares.

DACHAU

Grey skies,
Dark dirty buildings,
Chimney stacks, thrusting themselves
Towards the heavens,
And the never ending trains.
Bedraggled, hopeless people,
Exhausted, walking corpses
Marching, staggering
Towards the showers,
Towards the ovens,
Towards eternity.

Lucifer has fallen.
The shining light of heaven,
The mirror image of God,
His true son,
Sent to this wilderness,
This nightmare planet
To sort out souls.
Robbed of all awareness.
Not knowing his identity,
Relentlessly pursuing destruction.

You had no comprehension
Of your true name, or your destiny.
Perhaps you were a saint,
Procuring the salvation
Of countless souls.
Adolph Hitler, Lucifer,
You fulfilled your sacred task.
You took away their earthly ties.
You washed away their sins.
You burnt away their bodies,

Freeing their souls.
Adolph, you did well.
Those who endured the flames
Were freed forever.
Those who escaped your tender loving care
Must still face death,
The gateway to eternity.
Lingering for useless years
On dreary railway stations,
They wait for trains,
And for the final journey
To Dachau.

Don't Look Back

We are supposed
To learn from the past
But seldom do.
Same traps, same solutions.
We just get better and better
At making the same mistakes.

Like Janus,
We have two faces.
One looks forward,
One backwards.
We have no choice,
We must go forward.
It is too dangerous
To live in the past.

Lot's wife tried it.
Fleeing from
Sodom ,
She looked back.
She turned into a pillar of salt.
Lot's fate wasn't not much better.
Governed by
Perceived necessity
And Sodomese morality,
Believing they were
The sole survivors
Of Humanity,
Lot's daughters made sure
Their father was drunk
And stole his sperm.

The fate of Orpheus
Was also blighted.
Eurydice ,
Whom he worshipped,
Released to him
From Hades,
On the promise
He would show no distrust
By looking back.
He did,
Losing her forever.

Don't look back.
It gains you nothing
It anchors you
In waters
Which cannot
Be retraced.

Bring what you must
From the past
Into the present
But you can't navigate you boat
Unaware of the dangers
You currently face.

Darkness

Some fear darkness.
Perhaps they need
The reassurance
Of a visible word
To orientate themselves
To conquer isolation.

I can't see it that way.
Darkness is a warm blanket,
Giving me the chance
To discover me inner self,
To escape my boundaries.

Darkness embraces me.
She comforts me.
She holds me in her hands.
She is a life jacket,
Allowing me to float
In a stormy sea.

Equating darkness
With negative aspects of life,
Dark thoughts,
The dark ages,
Denies us
The opportunity
Of spiritual growth.

She will forever
Be my friend.
I cannot deny
The other side of existence,
But I welcome
The balance, which she offers me.

Dreaming Of You

I really tried to go to sleep
But that was not to be.
My thoughts, I thought would make me weep,
No comfort there for me.
I sleep, I dream, I dream of you.
I see you as I wake.
I know the image can't be true.
Your touch would surely make
My wildest dream reality
If that will be, my fate.
This mortal life is not for me.
I find it hard to wait.
My song is without melody
I would my flesh decay.
My spirit aching to be free
My flesh is in the way.
I know the time will surely come,
Our time on Earth is brief.
Until that time my soul is numb.
My heart is full of grief.

Dora

Dora was in high school
When she got hooked on drugs.
Thought it was oh so cool
To buy her fix from thugs.
She ran out of money,
What else was there to do?
Offered to sell honey.
The boys would form a queue.
All of them infected,
The honey laced with AIDS.
No statues erected.
No victory parades.

Elaine

I remember Elaine.
How could I forget?
I saw her play a double game
From when met
Until she died.
We met when
She was fourteen.
Whilst I was six months older.
We both were virgins.
She was tired of playing games.
She left me for another.
She offered words of
Consolation.
'He was so much like you
But we had sex
And you were much too scared.'
So many lovers.
So many husbands.
But never a child.
We both were lawyers.
I was at the Bar.
We shadowed
Each other's lives
On parallel tracks.
When I was forty three
We met again,
Both between marriages.
It was torrid affair.
She noticed
I was no longer frightened

After two weeks,
A note.
She needed time to think.
We met again two years later.
She'd been to Germany,
Another husband in tow.
He was bisexual.
Riddled with aids
She also.
Some things can never be
But how can I forget her
Or her choice of suicide

Emotion

I despair.
I cannot understand.
I see emotion on display
In every aspect of life.
I trust the poet,
In tune with feelings,
Describing them,
Freely admitting to his own
Or that which he perceives.
Love consummated.
Love lost.
Love never experienced.
Lust and passion.
Hatred and
Revulsion.
It is all there
In front of you.
Cruelty sadism.
Longing and fear.

Where does it reside in us?
Is it the soul or the flesh?
Sometimes our bodies
Are shaped in such a way
That we cannot satisfy
Our needs.
Cyrano de Bergerac
The hunchback
Of Notre Dame
All suffered
Because of faulty flesh.

The soul is there to learn
Not to have wants and needs.
It is our flesh
Which dictates
Our direction,
The direction of the species.
Morality
Has little to do with it.
We live and die,
We fight and lust,
Protecting our selves,
What ever that means,
And in the process
Perhaps the soul
Will learn a little.

For us,
The world is
A colosseum.
We are gladiators
Striving to live,
Not afraid to kill
When we must.
Hoping
That a kindly Emperor
Will point his thumb
Towards the heavens.

Enoch

Enoch appeared. He spoke to me
I clearly heard him say
"We spoke when you were only three
You slept the night away"

Now that you have turned twenty five
It's time to let you know,
A guard elf helps lets you survive
Wherever you may go.

A Guardian angel should be there
To guard humanity.
But at your birth, there was no spare,
So they commissioned me.

I might not have those lovely wings.
I wear a funny hat.
My fingers full of golden rings.
My face looks like a cat.

Don't be afraid, throughout your life
Your troubles will be few
I will be there in times of strife
I will look after you."

Empty Pages

Well here you are again.
I think you're looking a me
But I can't see eyes.
I don't know whether
You are smiling at me,
Or smirking in a superior
Manner.
All I see is a blank page
Challenging me
To say something meaningful,
Or shut off
The computer.

I heard you call.
My ears are finely tuned
To hear your silent
Voice.
What will it be?
Love?
Lost or requited,
Perhaps a little
Dig at religion.
It does no harm
To be a little cheeky
With a tolerant father
Some fathers, I hear
Are so easily offended.
What about politics?
The laws of treason
Don't seem to matter
Much today.

Perhaps I should
Do the usual thing,
Go into a trance
Like Madame Arkarty.
My familiar will do the writing.
Should I wait
For the odd Archangel
To dictate the words
To me?

None of that
Will happen.
My fingers will dance
On the keyboard
And new life
Will grace your
White emptiness.
You and I together
Progenitors of life.
By the way,
Do you know.
I love you?

Fairy Tales

They may be only fairy tales
But what they have to say
Applies to life as it prevails
Right to this very day.
The story of Red Riding Hood
Is one, which should be understood.

There was a kindly messenger
Supplying lots of food.
A predator had noticed her
And thought he would intrude.
Get rid of those with real need
And aim to satisfy his greed.

That is the way with foreign aid.
The poor will stay that way.
After the predators are paid,
The poor get none that day.
The fairy tale might turn out well,
The worldwide poor can to to hell.

Frustration.

I planned to do some writing.

My words could not be found.

The sea was so inviting,

They jumped in and they drowned.

They didn't realise the sea

Was called the lake of Apathy.

Fundamentalism

The twentieth century
Was a time
Of political decay,
Fundamentalism.
Isms had captured the imagination
Of the multitudes.
Madness captured active minds.
The right wing or the left,
It didn't matter.
Ideologists held power.
The Masses manipulated
Or killed.
All in the name of power.
Morality and decency
Had died.

There was an interlude,
When power passed
To others.
American plutocracy,
Organized crime.
All nationalities took part.

Then fundamentalism
Found a second wind.
This time religion.
No different
From their political
Predecessors.

The Christian brand
Was nothing new.
The Inquisition.
The Salem Debacle.
The Bible Belt.
Death meted out
By superstition.

Islamic fundamentalism
Rules
The new century,
Claiming lives ,
Threatening to invade
The world.

Jewish fundamentalism
Threatens
Israel's modernity
More friendly
With their Moslem counterparts
Than with the state.

It only needs an ideology
To marshal evil minds,
To justify disgusting deeds,
To give power
To the charismatic few
And leave mankind in fear,
To suffer and to die.

No people
Are immune
From this contagion.
No ideology is free
From such manipulation.

Power is shared
By plutocrats and corporations,
By men in fancy dress,
Military and men in holy orders.
As for the rest,
Well, losers can please themselves,
If not arrested.

Garden Gnomes

There was this guy called Abraham

Who thought it was his job to slam

The statues people would display,

The ones to whom they used to pray.

The household gods were quite upset.

They'd never faced this kind of threat.

They knew their jobs were on the line

Because Abe said they weren't divine.

A union meeting, organized.

The household gods soon realized

The best solution to be found

Was for them to go underground.

No matter what old Abe might say,

They just refused to go away.

And to this day you still can see

Them guard their household territory.

With happy smiles, around your homes

Disguised as quaint old garden gnomes

God Save Me

God save me from the rich,
Who hardly know that I exist,
Who pay little tax,
Whose children can avoid the draft,
Whist others die to save their wealth.
They sold the crops of Ireland
Overseas,
Whilst Irishmen starved.

God save me from the poor
Who cannot rise above
Their fate.
Drugs alcohol and sex
Don't help.

They help themselves
And often land in goal.
Their violence,
Though understandable,
Is indiscriminate.

God save me from the preacher,
Be he religious or political,
Who teaches his followers
That they are different,
That they are better,
That they are more entitled.

So many suffer the delusion
They are chosen people,
Chosen by God,
Chosen by geography,
Chosen by superior genes,
Whatever.

This gives them to right
To deal with lesser folk.
Dehumanise, destroy,
Accumulate their wealth,
Their heritage.
Destroy their culture,
Their bodies.

God save me from myself,
Recognizing human nature
Without doing anything
To make changes.
Interested only in my survival.

To stand by
In the face of so much evil
Is to endorse that evil.
The decision is self evident.
Which part of Self prevails,
My flesh or my beliefs?
How strong am I?

I am told that
Meek shall inherit the Earth.
I am still waiting
For my inheritance.

God Bless America

God bless America
The country of the free.
Where would be presidents so far
Requires a money tree.

It isn't a democracy.
To run for president,
It's only the plutocracy
Who raise the money spent.

The power will inevitably
Be held in wealthy hands.
The needs of folk like you and me.
Nobody understands.

The chosen people you are not.
Voters don't have a clue.
You guard the wealth, which you have got.
The poor don't get as sou.

So let the world stand back and clap
The land of superman.
The propaganda is just crap.
You'll gather I'm no fan.

Giving Birth

Ladies!
I recognise who you are.
You are the temples of Gaia.
Within you the altars,
Where sperm and ovum
Join to become
A life.
You have the gift
Of creation.

But it's not that simple.
I too give birth
As do countless others,
Men and women.
We give birth
To creations of our own.
Poetry and other works of art.

They flow from us,
Conceived in our imagination,
Growing and maturing
In readiness for birth.
Brought to life
By the ghosts
Who inhabit us.
Those who inspire us,
Memories,
Fantasies,
Conscious and
Unconscious.

Some are born
In pain and sorrow.
Some are stillborn.
Some have an essence of Beauty.
Some plain and dull.
Some are clearly
Our own children.
Some bear the markings
Of the ghost
Who planted the seed.

I must present my creations,
To you, who will
Help to sort them out.
My poems are my children.
They stem from my fertility.
They are my ambassadors
To all those
Who would share
My world
With me.

Gaia's Gift

Gaia, mistress of the Earth,
Who works with the Creator.
You have given us temples.
Each cared for and protected
By a priestess,
Jealously guarding the altar
Hidden in the depths
Of the temple.
A corridor
Leads to the altar,
The entrance hidden
In a mossy glen

The chosen are invited
To make the sacred journey.
They lay their offering
Upon the altar.
If Gaia rejoices in the gift
Life is created.
The Creator
Endows that life
With his own blessing,
The soul.

Hurstville 1996

Young faces, old faces,
Sleek black hair and slanting eyes.
Half-grown youths with baseball caps,
Elegantly back to front.
Merchants lounging by their doors.
The shops are full of merchandise,
But Customers have stayed away.

Groups dressed in tattered uniforms.
Pimply-faced boys leering at girls,
Seduction without aptitude,
Crowding the footpaths, smoking "grass.".
Timid young cops, straight out of school,
A shrunken version of the past,
Uncertain what to do.

Black faces, white faces,
Afro, Indian, Islander.
Glorious bodies full of strength
Or, perhaps a fatter form.
Women, young girls and their babies
Walk about with covered heads
Wondering why people stare.

A drunk or two, some casks of wine.
They lie at bus stops unperturbed
By signs forbidding alcohol.
An old man and perhaps his wife
Are heading for the local club
Whilst business men with faceless masks
Meander back to work.

Familiar faces, strange faces.
There was a time I knew them all.
It was a small community.
I walked the streets and waved to friends.
Those days are gone.
I am an alien in a changing world
Lost in a, multicultural universe.

Homecoming

I did return to Austria,
My birthplace.
My country of origin.
My oppressor.
A country, which gave birth
To terror and death.
It was more than sixty years
Until I overcame
My negativity,
My memory of
The fear, which consumed me
When I left.

I found a city
Which I did not know.
A people polite
To the tourist
Waiting to extract his cash.
I saw the usual landmarks.
I visited the street
The house where I had lived,
But hidden amongst
Beautiful new buildings
There was the shabby neglect
Of yesteryears' buildings
I feared that behind the glitz
Of newly fashioned platitudes
I would find the shabby neglect
Of yesteryears prejudices
Hatreds, suspicions.

And so it was
My Austrian German
Had survived
Years of neglect.
I spoke with taxi drivers,
With men I met
In pubs
Or their equivalent.
Nothing had changed
Other groups shared
The opprobrium.
Same clothes
On new bodies
But plenty left
For yesterdays
Object of hate
No, not yesterday
Today and tomorrow

I was not surprised.
I was tapping into
Old fears,
The wish to protect
Their own,
Whoever that might be.
To eliminate
The other
The usurper
The thief
Who comes to steal?
His holy heritage.

Old Wine

I was glad to return home,
Whatever that might mean.
Where ever that was.
I realised that
In a species of carnivores
Outsiders
Would always be
On the menu.

Haemophiliac

Like a haemophiliac,
I bleed,
Not drops of blood
But the elixir which
Flows from my soul,
From every pore
Of my existence.
Some emerges as tears.
Some as sweat,
When I am lost in lust.

I am in love
With all creation.
Nature has provided a feast,
To nourish me.
Each morsel
Absorbed.
I am reinvented
In the image
Of my maker.
Although my body fails,
I am immortal.
He takes my hand
And we fly
To other levels
Of existence.
I exude the ecstasy
Of sharing
In the greatest
Adventure of all times.

Helen Of Troy

Helen of Troy has always been
A symbol and a mystery.
Never before such beauty seen
It changed the course of history.
What was the source of her appeal?
How much was legend, how much real?

Helen, I think was my first love,
An adolescent fantasy
Raised Helen's stature far above
Mere mortals who might fancy me.
All men would risk their lives and sail
To Troy to rescue her from gaol.

Poor Helen never really knew
The reasons Greek ships put to sea.
The lust proclaimed by all the crew
Was really somewhat mercenary.
For beauty no one gave a hoot.
Troy had the wealth, they wanted loot.

But fate would further stir the pot.
Now we can very clearly see
That even Grecian greed was not
The reason of that victory.
Troy was the womb from which was torn
A glorious infant, Rome was born.

So rest in peace, Helen my dear
Enjoy the dream which dying brings.
We cannot know why we are here,
Our purpose in the scheme of things.
Of course, all men have worshipped you.
I must confess that I do too.

Dr. John R. Strum

In Troubled Waters

In tranquil waters, there I lie.
A quiet bay close to the shore.
A rocky border making way
For golden sand, a fine display.
I dream, as I am waiting for
The years to gently pass me by.
I am serene I shed no tears,
For I have known wonderful years.

My timbers not always the same.
I've needed refits over time.
I've carried loads, provided joys
For families with girls and boys.
Some times of grief and some sublime.
Always the oceans there to tame.
My families knew I was there.
All troubles would be mine to share.

I know that I am growing old.
My sails need mending, timbers rot.
My days are numbered, but I cope
Secured to buoys by sturdy rope.
If they don't break, no matter what,
I can survive as life unfolds
I float and I recall the time
When I was proud and in my prime.

The storm clouds, worse than I had known,
Creating havoc with the sea.
I knew my life would be at stake
If either of two ropes would break.
A storm of such intensity,
That on the rocks I would be thrown,
Or I would perish far from shore.
A wreck upon the ocean floor.

This angry storm I can't ignore.
The foaming waves crash down on me.
The ropes were never strong enough
To deal with oceans quite so rough.
If they should snap, my fate will be
To perish, thrown against the shore
My destiny may yet dictate
The lines will break and seal my fate.

I-WRITE-O-MANIA

I think it's time that I explain
The reason why I write.
I feel a drive within my brain
Which plagues me day and night.
I don't believe I have the task
Of spreading new ideas.
I don't believe that I will bask
In glory fit for seers.
I let you share my fantasy,
I don't pretend to know
What others really think of me.
It's just another show.
Sometimes my poems entertain.
Sometimes they may distress.
Some give pleasure some cause pain.
Sometimes it's just a mess.
Perhaps we play a childish game,
The game a child adores.
I'll show you mine, I have no shame
If you will show yours.
You realise I do not speak
About anatomy.
It's sharing of our souls I seek,
Comparing poetry.

In Ancient Times

In ancient times
Sacrifice usually
Spilt the blood of others
A person, usually a captive
Or a slave
Or a child
There were other gifts
Which could be made
Flowers crops
Produce.
But in most cases
A life was taken
Never the life of the one
Who made the sacrifice.

Why would anyone
Believe in such
Monstrous gods?
Not the givers of life.
The takers of life.

A different story today
Or is it,
Men kill for their beliefs
Or is it an excuse
A chance to kill
To plunder
To rape
In the name whatever
Belief you have.

In Love

In the ocean
Of emotion.
Touching gliding,
No more waiting.
So elating.
We are sliding
Deeper deeper,
Hiding
From the earth above .
We can feel
A love abiding.
Transformation.
Satiation.
Pure elation.
This is real,
This is love.
Make it last a little longer.
I know we can be much stronger.
I despair!
We must have air.
We must leave the sea behind us.
There will always be reminders.
Times of total ecstasy.
You and me,
In the sea,
In the sea,
Loving you
In the sea.

Iolanthe

I loved you
From the first moment
My eyes consumed
Your loveliness.
We did not meet Til later.
It was a sensual love,
A tingling of the flesh,
Insanity. Obsession.
I could think of nothing else.
Overwhelmed by my emotions.
I feared that I would lose control.
I would be swept out to sea
Into an ocean full of passion
Where I would drown.
I found it hard to breathe.
The world had changed.
Nothing else existed or mattered.
I wanted to touch you,
To be absorbed into the soften of your flesh,
Without really knowing
The nature
Of my desire.
My textbooks
Became a jumbled mix
Of letters,
An alphabet soup.
I wanted to write to you,
Poetry perhaps,
Not knowing what to say,

How to say it.
I didn't even know your name
Or where you lived.
I dreamed that night
That we were together
Sharing a bed,
Sharing a dream.
I was fifteen.
Ignorant.
Terrified
You would discovery
My ineptitude
And laugh at me.
That was twenty years ago.
We are still together.
We still share dreams.
I am as much in love as ever.

John Straede
(Astronomer)

It was a night of quiet conversation.
Two people sharing drinks,
Wondering about the universe.
You had your occupation,
Gazing into the heavens,
Trying to reveal the Face of God.

"It is stranger than you think"
You said, looking into the flames
Dancing within an ancient fireplace.
"We are merely children
Peeping through a keyhole
At mysteries beyond our comprehension."

"I do not find myself
Peeping through keyholes
John Straede."
Was my reply
"I contemplate my inner world
I marvel at the mysteries.
The stars, the separating darkness,
Exist inside of me.
The heavens mirror my soul.

Kel

He ate sausages in the park.
Each day he sat beside the well.
A distant and a vacant stare,
Alone, unwashed with filthy hair
People would comment on the smell.
He did not move, from dawn to dark.
He told me that his name was Kel.
He said that he had been abused.
He rarely heard what others said,
Only the voices in his head
The same words that his parents used
He could hear Satan's voice as well.
When local people did complain,.
Policemen would take him away.
He'd be admitted and receive
More needles than one could believe.
When beds were needed the next day,
They'd send him on his way again.
One day I saw that he was gone.
I heard from someone he had died
A service had been held somewhere.
Only the local priest was there
Nobody grieved, nobody cried
Without a ripple, life went on.

Living A Life

I have spent one lousy lifetime,
Crawling along a road
Leading to a hole in the ground.
Why?
Is there somebody watching?
Cheering?
Is it only myself?
If I were on a higher plane,
Looking down,
Perhaps it would all make sense.
I would understand
The destinations
Where other choices
Would have led me.
I would see the future
Of other relationships.
And yet and yet,
I know that it was inevitable.
I would have made the same
Choices again.
What am I?
An actor whose
Script was written for him,
By an unknown scribbler,
To be performed
For an invisible audience
Which cannot comprehend.
I am taking part in a play
Which will never
Be performed again.

Linked In Communication

The time is short the time is sweet.
I sit before my books and cram.
So many people yet to meet.
Before I face the great exam.
So much of nature to explore.
Mountains of knowledge I must gain.
So many lovers who will pour
Their feelings out both joy and pain.
So many people who will preach
Their deeply held religious view.
I know they only mean to teach.
I simply cannot join their queue.
The idealist has this to say.
'The world should be a better place'
And only he knows of the way,
And only he can judge the pace.
Some wish to heal the burning pain
Which they experienced in their youth.
So they will open wounds again
In order to find out the truth.
We live in countries far away.
I doubt if you will meet with me.
We are as one so let me say,
We offer help through poetry.

Last Night

Last night
Was rather quiet.
Everyone had gone to bed.
Only the puppies at my feet.
I listened for the call
Which greets me
When I wake
And in the evening.
My computer calling me.
Irresistibly,
Sometimes to the anger
Of my family.
I answer the call.
Tonight is different.
I can feel reserve
In our relationship.
I press wrong buttons.
The page I seek
Avoids me.
My computer demands
My attention.
I write and all is well

My Fantasy

The universe, we hold in awe
Was born from an explosive blast.
Where nothing existed before
A gaseous mass expanded fast.
A cloud from which the stars would form.
The planets and the galaxies
Created by that mighty storm.
Life then commenced on one of these.
The planet Earth would be the test.
Perhaps the only one so blessed.

We do not really comprehend
All the varieties of life.
We wonder what did God intend
When he produced this world of strife.
He needed bodies which would be
The wombs which gave birth to the soul
Which did not know their destiny.
The particles linked with the whole.
It seems creation had some use.
The means for God to reproduce,

God drifted on a different plane
Until he found he had the need
To render himself whole again.
For that he had to plant his seed
He found a void where he plugged in.
A stillness suited to his plan.
Creation ready to begin.
The final element was man
The real purpose was to be
Supply God's need for progeny

Of course he suffered jealousy.
It was his seed no plan to share.
He claimed there was no God but he,
But other gods were everywhere.
Out in the void looking for feeds,
Forming creations of there own.
On earth God only wanted creeds
Which clearly worshipped him alone.
The chance of losing souls was slim.
All newborn souls returned to him.

Beyond the earth the stars exist.
The void , a place where gods roam free.
Beyond the void there are the mists
And so until infinity.
Maybe existing at the end
There is the true God, the divine,
But mankind cannot comprehend.
So there it is now please feel free
To cobble your own fantasy.

My Journey

I cannot find the words,
I had once found so familiar.
Names escape me..
A thickening fog
Removes me from the world
As I had understood it.
I had been trapped
In a spider's web of words,
Logic, rules,

Ways of thinking
Which paid homage to beliefs
And patterns of thought
Dictated by society.
Political correctness.
Two dimensionality..

But now reality has changed.
It is no longer an organized mind
Which links me to the world
I feel the threads of fantasy
Creating new worlds.
Rivulets of new emotions
Attracting me to strangers
Lending comfort
To a sense of new discovery.

Old Wine

The shell is softening.
It is no longer possible
To differentiate
That which is within the shell
From that which exists outside.
My soul is caressing me,
Preparing me for a journey
To taste the infinite
To become one
With God

My Poetry

People who read my poetry
Say it is personal and deep.
I find it complementary,
I find it elementary.
I know full well I cannot keep
My inner self a mystery.
Although at times I must confess,
To plumb the depths, is to know less

I have lived life for many years.
The world has changed and so have I.
A trained spectator all my life,
A filter for the pain and strife
Of many people and I try
To deal with all their stress and tears.
Each person in my surgery
Took home a little part of me.

There have been benefits to me.
I am diminished. I have grown.
I've come to recognise the soul,
Without which nobody is whole.
Our flesh cannot survive alone.
We have to face eternity.
I can see beauty in all lives.
I grow with each one who survives.

My senses are the only guide
To what exists outside of me.
What I perceive is otherwise.
My sense of smell, my ears ,my eyes
Cannot know true reality.
To know the world I have relied
On inner truths I can't explain,
Tempered with happiness and pain.

My role in life has always been
To share my insights and my love,
Perhaps my writings will reveal
What I perceive and what I feel,
My inner dragons and my dove.
I will let everything be seen.
If I can make you think or smile
My time on Earth has been worthwhile.

My Eyes Are Hidden

My eyes are hidden
By an internal mirror
Reflecting back images.
Eager to break free
From the cauldron of creation.
Inside my brain.
Inside my soul.

I cannot tell
Whether I am seeing
The outer world,
Or merely
A reflection
Of my own.
Perhaps a mixture.

My ears are an antenna.
I long to hear some confirmation.
Are you out there?
Can you hear me?
Which message am I sending?
Is it a song about creation
Or merely distortions
I produce?

I hear your songs,
But is it my imagination?
Am I alone?
Or are we all part
Of one being?
Joined forever in the task
Of creating our universe.

My heart provides the drumbeat
So that we may march together,
Transcending isolation,
Cells of one body.
Each sentient
Serving other purposes
We may never fathom.

My soul is my companion
Waiting to be born
To Continue a journey
Which I will never make.
May my soul remember me
As one who served her well.

More About Helen Of Troy

Her face had launched a thousand ships.

Champagne did not exit in Greece .

A fractured nose and swollen lips,

Did not help in the cause of peace.

A fractured skull and broken teeth.

Paris had cast her from his bed.

Her bedroom now was underneath

The skies. The clouds dumped on her head.

For Helen, a calamity.

Her rivals sang and danced with joy.

Her lover Paris came to see

That he would rather have a boy.

It's quite OK to launch a craft.

It indicates that you have class,

But not your face that's really daft

It's better if you use another part of your anatomy.

Metaphors

I was listening to a lecture
At a seminar one day
When I had a sudden flash
When everything made sense
It was not a complex
Piece of knowledge I acquired
But so many things fell instantly into place
It was information obvious to those
Who considered it before.

'Psychotherapy' he said
' The art of the shared metaphor.'
Two creatures sheltered
By a crust which closed them in,
Isolated from each other
To protect themselves from pain.
Both attach to a medium
Which can break down barriers.
Both can grasp realities
Which have been concealed.
Like a spaceship which is docking
To a station out in space,
So that information
Goods and people can
Be shared
The shared Metaphor
Is the way souls
Can share each other

And so it is with poetry.
It is the gateway
For souls to enter
Into each others domain,
A way of communication
Understanding.
It is shared communication.
Breaking the shackles
Of the so-called real world.
So too with therapy
It is a healing process
Where pain and misconceptions
Can be cast a side.
Poet and recipient
Sharing the metaphor,
Can heal the past
Whilst promising a future.

Memoirs

The time has come

To write my memoirs.

Old enough to contemplate

Conclusion

Of a somewhat dull existence.

Young enough to have avoided

A visit

From Doctor Alzheimer.

An empty page before me

What can I say?

Do I really want prying eyes

Examining my failures?

I blush to think of them.

Successes?

Do I need to gloat?

I love the ordinariness

Of my life

Let it die with me.

Dr. John R. Strum

My Journey Into The Desert

I drove into the desert
To meditate.
They tell its been done before.
The sun makes you delirious
And so receptive.
Perhaps I'll come across
A burning Bush
Or fight an angel
On a ladder,
Or hear one dictate to me.
Perhaps I'll hear
Voices in my head
Telling me
'Your mother was seduced
And you are bastard born'.
Who can tell?
I felt the need.
Confused about identity,
About the purpose of life.
Perhaps I would die out there.
No one would ever know or care.
Perhaps like Buddha,
I would find enlightenment
And sit around
Until I put on all that weight.
Perhaps there was
Nothing to be learnt.
I would remain perplexed
But secure in my ordinariness.

Night Has Fallen

Night has fallen.
There may be stars,
Lighting up the skies
I would not know.
I can't bring myself to care.
I sit on a green sofa,
Two keeshonds at my side.
One snores but at least
She tells me
She is still alive.
No television to disturb me.
No ads repeated endlessly.
No people anywhere
Intruding on my reverie.

Without a conscious
Whisper of command
My hand reaches out
To my computer.
I will pass the time
With unknown friends
All dedicated to singing
In the heavenly choir.
The slow cascade of tones
Creating a world
Which only artists
Understand.
Such is the fruit
Of stillness.
Until the evening ends,
With utter weariness,
It is a time of blessing,
Of renewal, regeneration.
That is magic which I seek.

Nightmares

I can hear the howling of the wind.
I can feel the icy demons
Licking my face.
A blanket protects me.
I see the vast canyon
Of my mind.
The floor is covered by sand.
Tumbleweed is trying to
Escape their ravaging pursuers.
Little of value grows here,
Only the cacti, which I fear to touch.
There are the rocky walls
I dare not climb.
The creatures of the night
Threaten to devour me.
I hear voices, soothing
Comforting.Seductive.Hidden,
Whispering to me.
They claim to be angels,
Begging me to taste the cacti.
I know that If I could avoid
The poisoned spikes,
I could not avoid the poisoned fruit.
Can this be me ?
Although I am aware of it
Whilst sleeping,

The morning organises
My escape.
My defences seal off the invaders
Reassuring me
That all is not lost.
There is much more to me.
I can see
Sunshine, glorious birds,
Multi-coloured ,
Red blue green nesting in trees
Outside my window.
Green grass, tall trees and flowers.
I quell my fears and venture
Into the world again,
Until nightfall
When the nightmares
Will haunt me again.

Dr. John R. Strum

Oh Well You Can't Win Them All

When a body wants a body

What is one to do?

When my body wants your body

Trouble may ensue..

So, your body wants nobody

Even though I try.

I find other bodies shoddy

I'll sit down and cry

I don't care for anybody

You're the one for me

Please don't worry everybody

Please just let me be.

Peace In Our Time

History is a record
Of man's conflict.
The conquerors,
The conquered
Who don't matter.
Warriors, who change the landscape,
Collecting tribute
From the vanquished.
Driving their own people
Like pigs to slaughter
For the greater good
Of the Warlord.

The whole world is a temple.
No more sacrificing priests.
The true slaughterers
Are men in uniform
Or revolutionaries.
Human sacrifice,
To make the fields more fertile
Wealth into
Unworthy coffers.

Whoever heard of peace?
Was it Chamberlin
Who proclaimed
Peace in our time?
He was wrong,

As all of them are wrong.
Nobody fights for peace.
Only for survival.
How can it ever change?
This is who we are.
Whilst population increases,
Whilst there is less to share,
Any excuse suffices
To eliminate rivals.
Only the wealthy
Will get their reward
In this life.
Others rely on faith.
Feasting in Valhalla,
Virgins elsewhere.
Bodily needs met
When there is no body.

I hope there is a soul.
Otherwise,
We are actors
In a bad play,
To the hilarity
Of the gods.

Peter (before taking his medication)

My body is no longer mine.
It is wired.
The wires protruding from holes
All over my body.
Not blood but my life juices
Drip from my body,
Infusing the soil
With electricity
Which runs the turbines
Of creation.
The droplets fuse with root of trees
Giving voice to the fauna,
Taunting me,
Punishing me
For having revealed
Their true identity.
Branches, which are
Antennas,
Harvest messages
From ancestors
On distant planets,
Assuring them
Their time will come.

Dr. John R. Strum

I was once a human being
But now I am absorbed
Into a different sphere of creation.
I am a bridge
Between past and future
In my death
A miracle will happen.
The earth will be transformed
When the last of my fluid
Has melded with the earth.
All will change
The world will be at peace.

Robyn Lorraine at five

She was five and she was frightened.
Her dear brother used to say,
'You've been horrible today'.
And Her fears were further heightened.
He said she was Satan's prey.
He would steal and throw soul
Down into great black hole.

She was young but enterprising.
There were answers to be found.
She would dig deep in the ground.
She jumped in and not surprising,
She looked carefully around.
There was nothing there to find.
So she left her fears behind.

Robyn Lorraine

The children would play, but Robyn Lorraine

Was out in the playground, dancing again.

Nobody noticed the wonderful sound

Which delighted her ears. Robyn had found

A magical place, without any tears

Where elegant elves with very large ears

Admired her auras, dark brown and green

The colours of nature. She could be seen

By sprites and fairies, who would proclaim

Her exquisite beauty talent and fame.

They knew her life was spent in a dream.

In her next life, she would reign supreme.

Queen of all nature in heaven and earth.

Her rule would be marked by wisdom and mirth.

Banishing foolishness, evil and pain,

The world would be safe for children again.

Robyn Lorraine would find joy and romance

In a world made up of music and dance

We poor mortals not nearly as clever.

Would be her slaves and lover forever!

Robyn In The Garden

Today I saw her working,

Sweating but not distressed.

A smile on her face,

Gracing it with the glow of satisfaction.

She loves her garden

Which she shapes and nurtures.

She is an artist, a carver

Who cuts away the clutter

To reveal the intrinsic beauty

In the world around her.

Dr. John R. Strum

Robyn And Her Friends

She was sitting with her friends
(And the cat).
They had come to help her
Pack gifts
For the homeless,
For those who lived
In institutions.
When the job was finished
They sat happily
Sharing lunch.
There were smiles on all their faces,
They shared a bond,
Which lent magic to the scene.
I looked at her,
A stunning flower
In full bloom,
Filling the air
With a wonderful perfume.
All who inhaled
That wonderful fragrance
Were intoxicated.
Their souls
Danced to the rhythm
Of true love.

Robyn Lorraine A Love Song

I have never written any love songs
For you. It's strange in many ways.
The passion of my poetry belongs
To episodes from bygone days.
People have changed. Passions come to an end
It seemed so hard at times to comprehend.

I do not doubt the motives that inspire
The lovelorn poet to produce.
He may have lost the object of desire
Or merely sets out to seduce.
He dreams about the future or the past
Ephemeral lusting not designed to last.

We've shared a loving over thirty years
I know the beauty of your soul.
Your every mood, your laughter and your tears
You're real! No artificial role
Designed to mystify and to confuse.
We are ourselves. There's nothing we might lose.

So much about you, quite beyond compare
The sensuous beauty of your flesh.
The flaming tresses of your glorious hair
My weary spirit can refresh
Itself. The soft touch of your fingertips
Intoxicating nectar of your lips.

Your wisdom and capacity to care
Are qualities that I know well.
Your values, tough but scrupulously fair
So many ways that you excel
I've learnt so much. I've come to realise
The joy of life when two souls harmonise.

Dr. John R. Strum

I have no need for metaphors to draw
An image of the perfect you.
Impossible to love you any more
If fantasy were really true
If you were perfect, I would live in fear
My failings would prevent my coming near.

Were I to write a million songs or more
Each verse would echo but one theme
You are my life, the woman I adore
No need for fantasy or dream.
If fate decreed that I should live and love again
None would compare with you, Robyn Lorraine.

Rain

Blessed be the rain.
The parched soil
Quenches its thirst
And changes colour.
The flowers raise their heads,
Offering a prayer
Of thanksgiving.
The Almighty,
In the guise of clouds
Speaks to us
With booming voice
And touches all our senses.
In the drainpipes,
The frogs sing songs
Of praise
And children dance
In puddles.
Only the dog
Lies fearfully under the bed,
And the cycle
Of life and regeneration
Continues.

Dr. John R. Strum

Rainfall

It rained last night,
Sheeting down, like a vast shower.
No signs of gentle drops.
The heavens and the earth were joined,
Forming a unity.
One undivided entity.
It was the same
Yesterday
It rained
For three unremitting days.
I saw my world change.
The green grass was gone
And in its place,
water,
Lakes graced by the presence
Of delighted ducks.
I thought of Noah
But there was no sign
He would be needed..

I had worked in the garden,
Only a week ago.
There was a nest of ants.
I drowned them with my hose,
There was a hive of wasps.
I removed them with smoke and fire.

Gaia, invaded
By a parasite.
There is fire, There are floods.
The seas revolt against us
And the earth yawns
To swallow us.
We are the invaders, the infection.
Gaia fights for her survival
And we must hope for ours.

Dr. John R. Strum

Refections On A Cloudless Night Sky

I have always
Identified with the cosmos.
The dark matter is like
The unused capacity of our brains.
The explosive bursting of stars,
Destroying all in their paths,
Until the penitent dwarves
Sit and sulk
Somewhere in the heavens.
Nothing to show
For all that rage,
Echoes our own fury.
The nurseries of stars,
Reflects our own
Propensity to breed.
The black holes
Mirror our despair.

My greatest fascination
Is with the mass of
Twinkling Lights
Breaking up the darkness,
A curtain to keep prying eyes
From seeing God,
Broken up by billions
Of spy holes
For us to peek.
What we would see,
If we could,
Is beyond comprehension.

I do respect science,
A limited old man,
Bound by
Scientific method,
To consider only that
Which can be measured.

The light behind the screen
Which we perceive at night
Can only be seen
Through the eyes
Of fantasy,
Faith, and magic.
Worthless tools
To the scientist.

I look with wonder
Into the heavens,
Hoping to achieve
Some understanding
Of myself.
I am not concerned
With truths,
Only with those insights,
I alone can glean,
Offering me tranquillity
In a life of uncertainty.

Ringmaster

I did not want
To hear those words.
I Feared them.
Once spoken
The spell was broken.
When a tree is struck by lightening,
When it is enveloped in flames
It vanishes from existence,
The cinders remain
To fertilise the soil.
She left me. The show was over.

We recreated our own world,
A private circus
Shared by two people.
She, the ringmaster.
I performed
A multitude of roles
Our own wonderland
Where we could indulge
Our passions

I was a lion tamer,
My head inside
The Lion's mouth.
I was airborn,
riding on a ring.
I was a clown
With painted face.
There was much more .
I thought she was in charge,
Organising, planning,
Creating magic.

The words came from her lips.
"I will not play
These games with you.
I was never in control
All this was merely
your fantasy,
Your aberration."

Everything changed
The ring
Caught fire
The lion melted into
a puddle of snow.
The clown's mask
dribbled from his face
The tent was blown away
By wayward winds.

I was distraught.
My life destroyed,
Just like the fantasy.
That night I wept,
But in the morning
I knew
Another fantasy
would take its place.

Reality is a matter of Perception

It's all a matter of perception.
Reality exists.
We only know
The universe we have created.
A multitude of creations
Exist
Within a multitude of minds.
They are not cut off
From each other.
They can be reached.
They can be shared.
There are black holes in the heavens.
I do not know why they exist.
Perhaps they are the links
To other realms.
For us the channel
Is much simpler.
The gateways
For all to enter
Is
Poetry.

Rebecca

I saw Rebecca yesterday,

Walking in the park.

The sensuality of the way she walked,

As if dancing to a rhythm

Which only she could hear.

Two children walked beside her.

I was unable to breath,

Consumed with grief.

I wished she had not left me.

I wished the children were mine.

Stillness

There was stillness,
Despite the music of birds,
The wind hobnobbing
With the trees,
Humanity proclaiming
Delusions of dominance
Over the world,
The sounds of children
And cars.

The stillness persisted.
No comfort
To be found.
I was trapped
Inside invisible walls,
Unable to find solace
In the warm ebb and flow
Of the warm waters
Which bathed my soul.

I listened with envy.
Intoxicated people
In love with different gods,
parading like contestants
In a beauty contest.
Screaming , imploring.
'Pick me pick me
The other candidates
Are flawed.'

Standing By The Sea

I saw you standing by the sea.
How could I forget
The sinuous muscles of your body,
Glistened with gleaming sweat.
Strong pillars, support a pedestal
Exploding into wondrous dimensions
A loving heart is cradled within.
Your eyes, a promise of paradise.

There was a time,
My soul was made of ice.
Devoid of feelings.
I was alone.
The blazing passions of our love
Altered destiny.
We melted into each other,
Becoming one.

Lost in the magic
Of contrasting shapes,
Our loins embrace
We renewed
Our strength.
My eyes
Devoured your flesh,
My nostrils
Inhaled your soul!
You filled me
With magical energy.
I was a ship rushing
To embrace the stars.
I danced. I sang.
The songs of destiny

Dr. John R. Strum

Speculations Of An Insomniac

I know you've heard it all before.
It preoccupies me.
They are idiosyncratic thoughts.
We all have our odd way of thinking.
Thank God, no Inquisition around.

I cannot believe
That our God
Is the ultimate creator.
Don't mistake me,
An ultimate creator does exist,
Beyond our comprehension.
And we are
Superfluous to his needs.
He has no wish for
Adulation from
Insignificant creatures
.

Our God
Is also a creation.
How many levels
Removed from the ultimate
We cannot know or comprehend.
He too must survive.
His days are limited
By the expansion of the Universe.

Some More Satanic Verses
The Big Bang Theory Revisited
(a poem without rhyme or reason)

I look at ancient history.
There is a pattern to be found.
Two sons are struggling for a crown.
The younger one will win the day.
A mother's love will overcome
An aging father's true desire.

Man is a mirror of the Gods,
reflecting struggles which took place
In Heaven and on Mount Olymp.
Brothers who sought their father's love.
The winner to succeed his sire.
The looser would be cast aside.

It came to pass, the Unnamed God
Created two ambitious sons.
The older, Satan was the heir,
But Yahwe had his mother's love.
A fierce battle would be fought.
Yahwe would win Satan cast out

The fall of Satan would create
A cataclysm, a rebirth.
A universe emerging from
That mighty and explosive force,
A universe which would consist
of Satan's molecules alone.

Dr. John R. Strum

Sleeping With You

Hold my hand.
Let me look at you,
Sleeping in my arms.
There is a smile upon your face
And I wonder
Where you are.
Are you Astral travelling?
Where have your dreams
Taken you
Tonight?

I find it hard to sleep.
Each moment,
When I travel
Away from you
Is painful.

Our shortened lives
Are like a scenic tour.
Each incident
Each joy and disappointment
Are stops along the way.
We visit and for a little while
Deal with the pantomime
Which we encounter.

Old Wine

My dreams are mine
Yours are yours.
Such a large
Portion of our lives
We cannot share.
At last I fall asleep.
I dream of you,
But it is not the same.
I look at you.
I am breathless
Seeing your beauty.

Morning will come.
The dogs asleep
Beside our bed
Will call us
Demanding their breakfast.
The new day heralds
Another link
In the tapestry of our lives.

Dr. John R. Strum

Ships Which Pass in the Night

He was a judge.
I heard him speak
The day that he was elevated
To the bench.
He paid his way through law school
By driving taxis.
He told us of a fare
He picked up for a journey,
An older woman going home.
He took on board
A younger woman
Heading in
The same direction.
After a while
Youth turned to age
And said.
'You don't know me
But I remember you.
You are my mother
Who left us
So many years ago.
Age said to youth
'I think you're right'
Not another word was spoken
Until they alighted
In different suburbs.
And went their separate way.

Seascape

A small boat,
Sails flapping in a hostile wind.
Waves like angry jaws,
Clutching at the fragile vessel.
Blue-green monsters,
Capped with dirty foam,
Like an epileptic giant
Bent on destruction.

There were predators
Below the waves,
Waiting to devour
The human remnants.
Sailors, dazed and terrified,
Knowing they would not survive.

In the evening,
The was a stillness
Reaching out
To the contours of the earth.
Only the seabirds could be heard,
Screeching out,
Diving in search of food.

Salange

A name, which I had chosen.
A name, which has always
Echoed in my mind.
I would call out to her
But there was no reply,
Only an image
Looking back at me
From the deep caverns
Of my mind.
Her body was shiny black,
Glistening, A jewel.
She could have been
The Queen of Sheba.
Sometimes it was
Pale pink,
With bright red hair.
Eyes so blue,
Liquid pools,
Inviting an embrace,
A kiss.
At times she was petite
With mysterious
Oriental features.
We were bonded,
Coming from different
Spheres. Untouchable.
I was frightened
Of chasing her away.
My illusion bursting
Like a soap bubble
Leaving me bereft.

I would think of her
Sometimes
During the day.
It was at night
That she became alive.
It might start as a dream
But soon the magic of her body
Would occupy my bed.
I could smell exotic perfume.
Her breath
Had the aroma
Of roses,
Fresh from the garden.
The sheets would move,
Letting me know
I was not alone.
I heard a whisper
Calling my name,
Softly inviting,
Demanding my attention.
I would wake.
There was a fleeting image
In the corner of my eye,
Never clearly defined.
She would flee
Before I could capture her.
I wanted to drag her
Into a world other than her own.

Dr. John R. Strum

Is it a fantasy
Crafted by my needs?
Does she exist
In other dimensions,
Reaching out for me
Because she too
Wants me, needs me?
I like to think so
Two creatures
Finding communion.
No possibility
Of ever meeting.
But linked forever.

Sacrifice

In ancient times
Sacrifice usually
Spilt the blood of others.
A person, usually a captive
Or a slave
Or a child.
There were other gifts
Which could be made
Flowers crops
Produce.
But in most cases
Life was taken.
Never the life of the one
Who made the sacrifice.

Why would anyone
Believe in such
Monstrous gods,
Not the givers of life
But the takers of life?

A different story today.
Or is it,
Men kill for their beliefs,
Or is it an excuse.
A chance to kill
To plunder
To rape
In the name
Of whatever
Belief was held.

Some Thoughts About The Concept Of Self

Who am I?
What distinguishes
That which I recognize as me
From that which is foreign
Which I reject.
I have a name, but others share it.
I have a body
But it changes with the passing years
I was a baby and later a child
My body changes throughout adolescence
Until a man stared back at me
From the mirror
He could have been me
But left and right were inverted.
Now I have an aged form
Which has almost reached
Its use by date.
Ideas change.
Retirement robs me of identity.

Where can I find this entity?
The constant nucleus
Which defines me
Which governs my life.
Anatomists would fail
To locate it
It is part of my psyche
Which changes
In the course of my life.

It is made up of many lights
Which flicker on and off
Some are compatible with each other
Some in conflict.
Some cannot coexist
I am my body, my soul
I am my beliefs and my doubts
My friends and my enemies
My likes and dislikes.
Sometimes I must trade
My ambitions for my principles
My life for my beliefs
Or that of my family

Despite its potential
Instability
It is who I am
Although at any point of time
I may not be able to explain it
To others or to myself.

The Water Wheel

I had returned
To Mannersdorf.
The village, I once knew
Had changed.
All that remained
Was a dusty main street,
A bus stop
Where there was
A one-hour service
To the nearest city,
A deserted church
With neglected
Tombstones
Hidden by weeds,
A few houses,
Some side streets.

I wandered
Down a lane-way
Into another world.
Some well cared for
Fields and orchards,
A distant farmhouse,
Smoke coming from chimneys.
A swift running stream
Flowing through the landscape,
Graced by a water wheel.
The wheel rolled through
The water
Like an old man
Determined
To complete
An arduous task.

A shaft extended
Into a building,
Which grudgingly
Accepted the river's
Gift of power.
Grinding the grain
Producing the flour
For human sustenance

I sat under a tree.
I may have dosed.
It must have been a dream.
The stream was flowing,
Briskly, powerfully.
The wheel had grown
Into an enormous
Structure.
Emerging from the water.
Contained within the wheel
There was new life
Born from the waters,
Completing a cycle
And returning again
To a watery grave.

A pastoral symphony
Composed by
The supreme
Composer.
The small but mighty river
Nurturing the living,
Whilst taking part
In the cycle
Of life,
Giving meaning
To existence.

Dr. John R. Strum

Turtles As Role Models

I sometimes watch TV,
Not the crime shows,
They solve mysteries
Too quickly.
Their investigations
Interrupted
By advertisements
This was a nature show
About female turtles
And their offspring.
A female turtle
Waddled up the beach,
Selecting grains of sand
Which she could trust.
Her eggs were buried.
To be nurtured
By the sand,
Lovingly gently,
Until their time had come
And the sweet little critters
Braved the sand
To reach the sea,
Where they would
Have to avoid
The predators,
Eventually maturing
And continuing the cycle.

Of course very few babies
Made it to the waters.
Most were the delight
Of land born or air born
Predators.

Thus nature maintained
A balance
Which we humans
Try to avoid.

There is another balance
To be maintained.
God implants souls
Into each living
Body.
What if not all of them
Survived?
What if the shell,
The human guardian
Lacked strength,
Unable to protect them
From predators.
Not all would survive
To return to the ocean
Perhaps most would be lost,
Leaving the best
To find
Eternity.

The Traveler

There is a fire
Burning
In the centre
Of my being,
Consuming me.
Multiple emotions,
Some congruent,
Some in conflict
With each other.
I try to put out the flames
But that isn't
What I want.
I play a game
Akin to Russian roulette.
A child holding his hand
Into the flames
To test his immortality.
I want
That which I cannot have.
I have that which I do not want.
I scream out
Into the night.
Knowing that my cries
Are muffled.
I walk the streets,
Invisible.
I seek to touch strangers,
But they cannot feel my touch.
Perhaps I have traveled
From the future
Or the past.
Perhaps
I will never know.

Trains

I live.

I breath I recognize my feelings.
I hear, l see. There is universe out there
Beyond my reach.
Somewhere, inside my head
An invisible computer.
A private internet. Messages flooding in
A code I must unravel.
I think I understand the world.
Perhaps it is a fantasy.

I know

There is a world out there.
I can predict responses to my probing.
I can locate the food I need,
The clothing to defeat the ravages of cold.
Sometimes I recognize the predator.
But I can never know the nature of the world

I love

There is no greater joy than loving you.
And yet there is a separation.
Although we seem to think alike,
I cannot think your thoughts.
I cannot feel your feelings.
We are, forever, prisoners within our skins
Within the essence of our being.
Although we share moments of ecstasy,
our unity is an illusion.

Dr. John R. Strum

I am

A passenger aboard a train.
Alone. Windows aplenty. Painted doors.
Mere daubs, No promise of escape.
I do not know from whence I came
I do not know my destination
Perhaps they are the same.

I see

A changing world through frosted glass
Breathtaking landscape, forbidding scarps
Happiness and tragedy.
Strangers who seem to share a common fate,
A world I cannot share.
I do not know who drives the train.
I only know that I have no control.
I sense my loneliness.
I fear and yet I crave my destination.

Toolumba Dreaming

I was dreaming of Toolumba.
We were innocent and young.
Half awake and half in slumber,
Melodies were left unsung

There were those who took their chances.
They were confident and sure.
Seeking you with furtive glances,
I felt foolish, insecure.

We believed we had the power
to control our destiny.
We believed this was the hour.
We would rewrite history.
No-one knew what would unfold.

Time goes by and nothing alters.
no-one knows what will unfold.
Dreams dissolve, ambition falters.
One thing happens, we grow old.

There are echoes of my passion.
There's a feeling memory.
I still care in my quaint fashion.
You're a special part of me.

The Tower Of Babel

The tower of Babel is destroyed.
Its stones lie scattered on the ground.
The demons gather, overjoyed
Despite the carnage, having found
Themselves alive. They have the power,
To desecrate and to devour.

A lynching in America.
A man accused. Outside the goal,
A frenzied crowd. No force can bar
Their entry. Evil will prevail.
The victim's corpse left on the ground.
proof of his guilt was never found.

A pogrom raging in Ukraine.
The houses burnt, the women raped.
And all the children have been slain.
No Jewish person has escaped.
Yet nobody had found it odd
To murder in the name of God.

The killing fields, the Nazi slime.
A lust for blood devoid of sense.
The same excuse used a every time,
The classic Nuremberg Defence.
"I know no evil, only love."
I followed orders from above.

How can it change? This is our fate.
We humans, gathered into groups..
Are easy to manipulate
Whilst Satan and his evil troops,
The scum of Babylon , still thrive,
How can Humanity survive?

To Sleep, To Dream

It was late
In the evening.
A black shawl
Adorned with twinkling lights
Hid the world from my eyes.
I did not know this world
In daylight hours.
Soon
I would be
Called away
To live another life.

Nothing felt the same.
There was
An all pervasive
Aura of strangeness.
Figures from my past,
From my future,
From other forms
Of existence,
Flittered in and out.
Past experiences
Were altered.
There were places,
Incidents revisited,
The only souvenirs
Which returned with me
Were feelings,
Anxiety, sadness

Sometimes joy.
My flesh, chained
In this reality.
My soul exploring
Alternates.
Sometimes relieved,
Sometimes unbearably
Sad to return.
I am not one.
I am a multitude,
Living a multitude of lives
In preparation
For what is to come.

This Is Your Life

I have searched the landscape,
The bushland and the beach.
I have sailed the oceans.
All to no avail.
I walked through cities
Canyons, windblown.
Buildings waiting to swallow
The unwary passerby.
Others are spat out.
I have seen the multitudes
On their way to somewhere,
Walking as a cohort,
Walking in isolation.

I have looked at God's creations.
The birds able to achieve
That which I cannot.
The soil invaded by insects,
Creating kingdoms
Ruled by females
Who kill off rivals,
Some devour the sperm donors.
Most Animals and fish,
Killing, eating, reproducing.

Dr. John R. Strum

I have been overawed
By trees and flowers
Producing the oxygen we breathe,
The fruit we eat.
Perhaps trees they are the true
Towers of Babel
Rooted in the ground
Never reaching heaven.

There ought to be a meaning.
It surely has a purpose.
 All I can discover
Are man made theories,
Lacking in credibility.
I need to know
Who I am. Where I am.
My desperation, however
 Must be tempered
With patience.
Perhaps in later lives
All will be clear.

The Wizard Of Oz

He was a little man

Controlling a great machine

The ultimate shaman

More sham than man

But he had the ability

To engage the power of dreams

And so

Dorothy returned to Kansas.

Dr. John R. Strum

The Voyage From Eden

Somewhere in the galaxy
There was another world.
A ship was there for all to see
Its banners were unfurled.
The message on the flag was clear
A three-hour trip through outer space.
Your journey set to start right here.
Be quick whilst there's a place.

The skipper of the ship was skilled.
His mate was Gilligan.
The ten seats on the boat were filled.
And so the trip began.
Amongst the passengers to leave
Were folk from different lands.
Also two called Adam and Eve
Computer in their hands.

Of course the skipper did not know
That Adam was a thief.
An Apple had been stolen, so
He fled to avoid grief.
There was a storm the boat was lost.
It landed here on Earth.
On shore the passengers were tossed.
Gilligan roared with mirth.

The two of them worked through the night.
The work went on apace.
The boat would turn out quite all right.
They blasted into space.
When they checked the passenger list,
Adam they could not find.
Adam and Eve had not been missed.
They had been left behind.

That is the way the myth began.
Computer thrown away.
That was the origin of Man,
Who lives here to this day
The skipper and poor Gilligan,
They finished up in goal
No more such cruises would they plan
When they got out on bail.

Dr. John R. Strum

The Streets Of Some Middle Eastern Town

You want to see folk overcome with joy?
You want to see them dancing in the street?
The rifle being held is not a toy.
You cannot tell what infidels you'll meet.

A lot of bullets shot into the air.
A passing flock of birds is terrified.
The shooter doesn't really seem to care.
No skill to hit them even if he tried.

What is it that is causing such delight?
Perhaps some drugs are being passed around.
Suicide bombers set a town alight.
So far, ninety-eight corpses have been found.

The more they kill the more they sing and dance.
The lives taken are causing no distress.
It only matters that their cause advance.
The rights of other people? Meaningless.

We have been told that we must not complain.
We're seen as rubbishing what they believe.
So it will happen many times again.
And they will sing and dance whilst others grieve.

The Omnipotence Of Childhood

I can do anything.
My mind is alive,
My imagination creates new worlds.
No power
Can undo my work.
No dream beyond my grasp.
I look into the mirror,
My body, young and virile.
Who can resist my charms?
Not I!
I hear the sounds of nature.
I see the multi-colored delights
Which God created for my pleasure.
Why am I less than He?
I have the power to create
A universe.
The past the future are
My playthings.

I mold them,
To amuse myself.
I am immortal.
There was no time before my birth.
I will not know a time to come.
I cannot think about my death.
Perhaps, one day.
A loss of innocence.
Realization That I am not
The centre of the universe.
Not now, perhaps never
I cannot, I will not
Contemplate the possibility.

The River

There was a vague outline
By the river's edge.
It may have been
A human Being.
It could have been me.
Perhaps
In another life.
There were echoes
Of memories,
Mere snippets,
People grieving,
Part of their life pattern
In tatters.
Hard to recognise.
They seemed so far away.
Emotion, mere shadows
Unlike any I recall.

The river was not a raging torrent.
It moved in a languid lazy way,
Coming from God knows where,
Going to the oceans of infinity.
The waters ,
If that is what they were,
A muddy hue.
Nothing could live there.

In the distance,
A shape hidden
Inside the folds
Of a grey shroud.
A smoky space

Where a face should
Peer out.
I could not make out
Arms or hands.
And yet
The craft was being driven
In my direction.
I knew that it would
Take me to the other shore.

I could not see
That side of the river.
It was hidden
By purple mists.
There was an oppressive
Silence.
Lifeless yet occupied.
I recognised my destination.
I was overcome with fear.
Looking back
At my life,
There was nothing I could change.
Idiosyncratic beliefs
Deeds best left undone.
On these
I would be judged.
I stepped onto the craft.
The boatman was silent.
What was left of me
Melted away .
Memories, mere shadows,
As I approached
My destiny.

Dr. John R. Strum

The Meaning Of Life

There is a job that must be done.
These precious cells, immortal seeds,
Need nurture so they stay alive.
So fragile and with special needs
I cannot salvage every one.
Only a few of them survive
Their journey through this universe,
Sharing their beast of burden's curse.

The reason I created man
Was as a mindless herd of mules.
The seed, implanted with the sperm
would be the one who made the rules.
It was a bonus to my plan
To see these mortal creatures squirm.
Thank God (that's me) they are so dumb
They think there is a Kingdom come.

The seedlings feed on human pain,
So I make sure that it abounds.
But I must feed the mules as well.
It's not as silly as it sounds.
They must believe there's much to gain
in seeking heaven, dodging hell.
They see me as a loving God
Who really cares for them. How odd

So now you have it, now you know
The secret meaning of it all.
There really is no mystery.
Your role is really very small.
Your purpose ending when you go.
You're useless in the cemetery
So pray to me and hold me dear.
Thank God I'm deaf, so I can't hear.

The Loss Of Love

The scientist says and rightly so
'That which I measure I can know.
I need to see the evidence.
I need to know the difference
Between myth and reality.
Research will split the two for me.'
Yet physicists say, sharing drinks,
'Physics is stranger than man thinks'.

Particles moving at a pace,
We never know their actual place.
Planets, one only knows each one
By watching wobbles of its sun.
More known about an iron rod
Than we can know about our God.
Particles, planets, we suspect
That they exist by their effect
On other bodies. If that's true,
Know God by his effect on you.

I know the joys that love can bring.
I lose myself. My soul will sing
My flesh will melt. I am reborn,
Lost in the light, a bright new dawn.
I know when love is lost to me,
But I have known eternity.
A God of love will be my fate.
I know my future. I can wait.

Dr. John R. Strum

I know I will survive my pain.
My soul will flourish once again.
The pain free life for which I yearn,
Not in this life .My soul must learn
Pain is the price which I must pay
To help my soul along the way.
But love is also there to teach
That God is never from my reach.

When love is lost please don't despair.
There always is someone to care.
Taste from the magic fruit and feel
The power of the fruit to heal.
May you regain the passions lost,
Despite the pain despite the cost.
You have been blessed. You have been shown
That you will never be alone.

The Human Plague

I do not presume
To understand nature.
The has a mind of her own.
She seeks to protect this earth
From destruction.
She admonishes
Living creatures
If they are intent
On destroying her beauty.
We hang onto her coattail
While she plays havoc
With her children.
Storms, floods ,earthquakes
Stop us becoming complacent.
Put us in our place

Nature can only deal with us
In manageable proportions.
Epidemics, the flooding of the
World with any species
Destroys planet
And creature alike.

We who are but grains of sand,
Making up a desert,
Wasting the land
Preventing other creatures
From flourishing,
Are not individuals,
For some benevolent force

Dr. John R. Strum

To care for each of us.
We are a mass
A beach who is swept away
If nature so decides .
The time will come
When nature takes
Direct action.

Peace is the breeding ground
For human plagues.
War is a way that nature deals
With excessive population growth.
Other plagues flourish
Amongst the masses
Hunger lack of supply
Will help control
The overgrowth
Of humanity.
It subsides
And we can start again,
Having learnt nothing
About the iron fist
With which nature rules
Its children.

The Haves And Have Nots

You couldn't even offer me
A lousy slice of bread.
You didn't like what you could see
And slammed the door instead.
You live inside your lovely place.
Your have these lovely wheels.
Your money comes at quite a pace,
With all those Wall Street deals.
The time will come.
There'll be a crash.
And then where will you be?
You will run out of all that cash,
And beg for food like me.

Dr. John R. Strum

The Gift of Poetry

Let me become an open book.
I want to share myself with you.
My thoughts and feelings, love and fear,
My inner soul, things I hold dear.
(Some things imagined some are true)
They're all displayed for you to look.

The world is merely metaphor.
A marvel, which we all create
Come read my words and share with me,
A majesty, a mystery
Together we participate.
In magic worlds, there to explore.

Just close your eyes and you will see
A stairway which we both can climb
To dizzy heights, where we can share
The beauty, which exists out there
The terrifying, the sublime
This is the gift of poetry.

The Forces Of Nature

During the rain storm,
Ribbons of water
Flowed through my garden
Towards the street.
Little lagoons of water
Were forming.
They would join,
To create a small inland sea.
Islands were scattered
In a beautiful pattern.
Some insects clung to
The safety of the soil
Whilst the pools teamed
With myriads of creatures
Swimming to reach a safe retreat.

It was a mini disaster.
Life was destroyed.
Their homes were lost.
The birds on high
Cried out in their triumph.
They fed on the creatures
Who had been
Exposed.

After a few days
The rain had stopped.
The sun bore down
Hardening the soil.
The birds were no longer
The scourge of the creatures
Who could not hide.
The feast was over.

The cycle of life
Continued.
The balance of nature
Endured.
People ventured
Out from their houses
To deal with the debris,
To repair what they could.

The crops, which they planted
In garden beds,
Beyond saving.
The flowers thoroughly
Drenched and crestfallen.
Some blooms survived
Attracting the bees.
For today there was water aplenty
Enough for their comfort.
Enough for their needs,
Not their safety.

A blessing for some
A disaster for others
The prickly nature of Nature
Prevailed.
We witness her tantrums.
We save what we can,
The rest washed away.

So little doubt who
Governs this planet.
We strut like heroes,
The rulers of earth.
The truth, is however the truth.
Like those poor drowning creatures
In greater disasters
We'd be swept away.

Against the power of nature
The power of prayer
Will be of little help.
Her outbursts prevail.
We must endure
And deal with her rages.
We nurture the Mother
As best that we can,
For nature herself
Cannot be conquered.
Our engineers
Perform mighty deeds,
But dams and bridges
Will fall to the torrents.
Earthquakes
Devour the houses
We have built.

We do what we must.
We count the victims.
We are grateful
To greet the survivors.
We continue our struggle,
Our fight for survival.
We build for the future
As best as we can.

Dr. John R. Strum

The Ending of the World

It's nothing new,
We've heard it all before.
The world will end,
Only the faithful will be saved.
A thread will guide them
To the Promised Land,
In less than forty years.
The day came and went,
The hour passed
And there was nothing.
The world was still intact
And free of rapture.
Somewhere a woman
Breathed a sigh of resignation
And went home to cook the dinner
She had hoped
Would not be needed.
The workers returned
To offices, to quarries
And a prophet went over
His calculations
And gave us yet another date.

The Coloseum

The schoolyard
Is a training field
Where lessons are taught
Not by any curriculum
Not with any intent
But because life
Is what it is.
In Life only the fittest
Will survive
The weak will find solace
On a psychiatrist's couch.
The meek may inherit the earth
But not the schoolyard
Not the world.
The bully serves a purpose
The victim needs explanation
To absorb the lesson
And so pass the tests
Life will throw up
In later years.

The Cave

I spent much time
Wandering in the bush.
I was an alien in this land.
A refugee
Who had learnt
The language
But not the ways
The culture, the beliefs
Of other children
Whom I met at school.
It had been a time of war.
We were enemy aliens,
Identifies with those
From whom
We had to flee.
I envied their home life
And perhaps their faith
With little understanding
Of my own.

For me the bush
Was a sanctuary.
Nobody to harass me.
A world of wonderful trees.
I could love.
They would caress me
When I climbed into
Their loving arms.
Secure they would not
Let me fall.

The gentle Breeze,
The fingers
Which would pluck the harp,
Teasing a voice
From the trees.
Melodies of love.
Of reassurance.
Multi-coloured birds.
I marvelled at their hues,
Red, green, blue.
Flying
From tree to tree.
Part of the choir.

I found a cave,
Not a hollow
Carved into the rock.
A large ledge
Giving Shelter to the
Undergrowth.
There were spider-webs.
I remembered
Last week's lesson,
Robert the Bruce.
I wondered whether the webs
Were spun to shield
Me from my oppressors,
But they existed only
In my mind.

I often returned
To my cave
To contemplate,
To find the courage
To get on with my life
To find myself.
It was a haven
Where I was
With my friends.

The day would come
When I would leave my womb
And continue building my life.
In my storehouse
Of memories,
I remember my cave
And the healing power
Of nature.

The Blue Mountains

When the morning mists had lifted,
I could see the valleys and the mountains,
Stretching out from cliffs
Which buttressed my house.
The mystery of the night
Gave way to the comfort of familiarity.
The ghosts which haunted
The Blue Mountains,
Retreated to their caves.
All that was left
Were the ghosts of past experiences,
Forever haunting me,
Pointing the finger
Laughing at my poor attempts
To live a life.

Dr. John R. Strum

The Blue Lady

Last night was different.
I am used to my dreams,
To my fantasies,
To waking in the middle of the night,
Thinking I had seen a face,
A shadow
Not clearly recognisable.
Clearly an echo of my dreams
Or wish fulfilment.
I have felt the pain of my visitors
And sometimes the delight.
We never touched ,
But there were shared feeling.
They came from
My dream world,
From my past or future
I loved them.

Last night was different.
I do not try
To understand.
I was awake
But my eyes were still closed.
I felt her presence
Close to my bed.
I debated with myself,
Half afraid of seeing her.
In an instant
My eyes opened
And there she was.

She was not anybody
I had seen before.
Her outlines were firm.
Her face familiar
Yet unknown to me.
Her age was indeterminate,
Her hair black,
But mostly hidden by a shawl.
She wore a blue robe.
She stood still,
Intently looking at me
Until she noticed
My eyes were open.
Then she withdrew
Sliding backwards
Until her form blurred
And she vanished.

I had felt pleasure
In the company
Of my nocturnal
Visitors.
I felt a sense of
Strangeness
With the Blue lady.
I know that
That she will come again.
Perhaps next time
We will touch or speak.

The Second Visit of The Blue Lady

I saw her at night.
She was standing near
My bed.
She fled.
When my eyes opened
I felt no fear
It was clear
Instead of bonding ,
She was absconding.

I had seen her face.
She had been dressed in blue.
She fled.
She vanished from my view
Leaving a mist,
An aura.
At the time I never knew
What had taken place.
In my world
It didn't' seem true.
But couldn't ignore her.

A strange idea
Formed in my mind.
Was she my guardian? Maybe
She came to guide me
To a boat
On which I'd float ,

To a distant shore,
To a destiny.
My life would be no more.
I had no fear.
She left behind
No feelings of any kind.
Only a certainty
She would return to me

There was a journey
Which I had to make.
I was tired.
I as not at liberty
To forsake
That trip.
I did not feel
Particularly inspired.
Wakefulness tended to slip
I woke before I hit the truck.
A monster painted blue.
Was it just luck?
It was surreal.
The monster had a name,
Blue lady was its claim to fame.
A female driver at the wheel.

I stopped and tried to think
Was this a dream ?
Or was I on the brink
Of meeting that weird
Apparition yet again?
I could have died.

Was I committing suicide?
My fuzzy thinking cleared
The time had not come when,
As I had feared,
I was to make the final trip.
It was important I should try
To hold onto my grip
Of sanity. I feared
The blue lady and I
Would meet another day
And then perhaps she'd have her way.

I do not know
How much is fantasy.
I do however think it's so.
Death comes for all, not just for me.
Perhaps the time had not been right.
The hour will come when I must go.
The boat will come and she will row.
My soul will vanish in the night.
Life must come to an end
I feel quite safe with my blue friend.

The Birth Of Religion
(satanic verses, three)

This universe first came to be
When out of paradise I fell.
The atoms which were part of me
Formed everything you now can see
And all the universe as well.

When all the pieces were in place,
I wanted to play games and so
I gave birth to the human race.
Those darlings, who would have my face,
Were cancers, which would spread and grow.

I ruled them with an iron rod.
The idiots thought they had free will.
Each one believed the path he trod
Ensured he was beloved by God.
All others there for him to kill.

Because the world was full of fools,
I had designed a special plan.
Different beliefs would be my tools.
Different religions, different schools.
And everywhere man would kill man.
Great priests and prophets would arise
To stand and preach the holy word.
Their rhetoric would hypnotize.
All other faiths made up of lies
With dogmas evil and absurd.

Dr. John R. Strum

The folk who dared to disagree
Could choose conversion or the sword.
I reveled in their misery.
A burning stake might set them free.
But only death was their reward.
Let all applaud my artistry!
I have created human kind.
They seek a loving deity,
But what they get is only me.
There's nothing else for them to find.

The Altar

The night was dark, a starless cloud,
Oppressive and cloying.
So difficult to breath or move.
A long line of black gowned figures
Slowly wending their way
Along a hidden path.
It was hard to see their shapes,
Impossible to know their sex,
To recognize their true identity.
Each face was shrouded.
Their hands were gloved.
Each was carrying a flaming torch.

I had some recollections,
Some memories of other times.
Flitting familiarity.
Friends and others I had known
Passing by, some that I had touched.
But not tonight.
I sensed the purpose of the journey.
This was a pilgrimage.
Deep into the woods to a hidden glade,
An altar and a sacrifice.

As we slowly made our way
Along that tortuous track,
The flames would flicker
One by one the lights would fail.
The shapes would fade, absorbed
Into the ever deepening darkness
Until I was alone,
Contemplating the true nature
Of my destination.

There was a clearing.
The trees made way to let me in.
I was alone yet I could feel
The company of hidden forces.
Before me, in the middle of the glade
I saw the altar.
Its call was irresistible.
I lay me down upon the stones
Awaiting execution, sacrifice

Where darkness ruled,
There was a shimmering.
The altar changed. There was a doorway
Where the stones had been.
I floated gently through that portal
Into another life.
The shrouded forms surrounded me,
Caressing me in joy and comfort.
I knew I had returned
To a long forgotten home.

The Alchemist

Poetry is alchemy.

Take out of the world

The ordinary.

Add a brew

Made up of

Words, emotions,

Imagination.

Stir

Within the reader's mind.

Turn carbon into diamonds

To adorn.

Turn lead into gold

To enrich.

Turn the ordinary

Into magic.

Dr. John R. Strum

The Adam Family

Adam. Who the hell was he?
No one knew from where he'd flown.
He had called it Paradise.
Never seen by human eyes,
Not all galaxies are known
It remains a mystery.

Took a woman when he fled.
They had both been charged with theft.
They stole fruit owned by the state.
Trial date set they couldn't wait.
Took their chances when they left
Settled down and interbred.

They had offspring, only two.
God knows where they found their wives.
Abel's cooking was just great
Cain's food used to constipate.
Eat the food and lose your lives
Cain knew what he had to do.
Cain wanted to win that round.
Such rejection hurt his pride
He thought he would win the day
Abel would be put away.
He invented fratricide
Everlasting fame was found

Moral of this tale, they say,
We have come from rotten seed.
They were murderers and thieves
Excuses no one believes.
Time has not improved the breed.
We are still like that today.

The Moving Finger

The moving finger writes.

God didn't have a pen.

He sometimes uses megabytes

And radio now and then.

It isn't up to me to judge

Just what he had to say.

All I could see, a great big smudge,

But, good try anyway!

Dr. John R. Strum

The Pied Pipers

(Homage to Poets)

I love the music

Of your language.

I love the magic of your themes.

You have a rich

Imagination.

I am entranced

By what I read and hear.

Your melodies

Resonate with me.

I want to dance

To your harmonies and rhythm.

You are surely

Pied pipers

And I follow

Spellbound, jealous

Of your talents.

Uniforms

I always thought
The purpose of a uniform
Was to distinguish
One group from another,
So in times of war
One won't be shot
By friendly fire.

Perhaps the uniforms,
Which are natural
To most creatures
Serves in the same way.

Identification
For the other
To attack or avoid,
To attract the opposite sex.

But it is far more than that
For mankind.
True, it is a message
For the other
But it is also
A message for myself.

I lose my loneliness.
I become part
Of something greater.
I am the army
And self pales into
Insignificance.

I am the choir
Not merely the choirboy.
The church
Not merely a man
Performing a task.

I melt into a multitude.
We are a union
Functioning as one.
I surrender individuality.
I do not have to know
Merely to accept.

I am a grain of sand.
I am the beach.
When I wear a uniform
I have changed my skin.
The borders
Of my ego stretch
Into the distance.
I have grown
Into a greater creature.

The glue
Which holds this entity
Together
Is a decision,
Not necessarily made by me,
That it shall come to pass.
Thereafter it is faith
Not reason
Which keeps me in my place.

Words On The Winds Of Change

The winds of change
Blow gently,
Or are so fierce
They carry all before them.
They can affect multitudes
Or individuals.
It may be an army
Accompanied by dust storms
Laying waste to countryside,
Destroying cities,
Enslaving those
Who have survived the sword.
If nature takes a hand,
Earthquakes and tsunamis.

There are more subtle winds.
Ideas and knowledge
Can render changes,
Perhaps more permanent,
Without generating
Instant regrowth.
A return to the status quo.
These are the winds
Created by words,
Written or spoken.

The spoken word
Which moves the heart
For good or evil.
The Sermon on the Mount,
Martin Luther King.
The rhetoric
Of Hitler.

Dr. John R. Strum

The written word
Born with
The printing press,
Which gave the word
Directly to all,
Without the need
Of interpretation.

The power of the word
Is mightier
Than the entropy
Of sterile cultures
Ways of life
Guarded by priests
Kings and millionaires.

Revolution
Comes and goes
All that changes
Is the bum on the seat
In a game of musical chairs

Man's basic nature
Does not change.
Some dust swirls.
Leaves and twigs
Are thrown around.
Sometimes cars and rooves,
But it settles down.

Are women really more equal
Than before?
Not in Araby.
Slavery still exists
The wealth gap widens.
Racial and Religious
Discrimination
Flourish.
Give the pot another stir,
It's still the same soup.

Words on the winds of change?
The suitcase has blown open
And as we chase the blowing pages
On which the words are writ.
The winds of change
Will blow them out of reach.
We will have to wait
For new teachings.

Why

Why do I have the compulsion to write?

My inner child is struggling to break free.

Why is it so hard to bare my feelings?

My passions are so strong they are dangerous.

Why do I hide behind a mask of seniority?

You may mistake my meanderings for wisdom.

Why do I look for other realities?

One reality is not enough to describe the infinite.

Why am I in love with nature?

Nature is the pen with which God writes

Why am I in love with you?

You are my magnet. You are my soulmate.

Welcome

To my creation.
Come and explore
A life different
From other lives
Other perceptions.
Expect the familiar,
Spiced with alien features
Which you might scorn.

Perhaps our souls
Will resonate.
Perhaps the song we sing
Will be the same.
We will be dancers
Around a maypole
Our ribbons.
Weaving wonders
Which can be seen
Only from above.
We see the stars
Twinkling above us
The stars
Which are the substance
Of the soul
In between, another strata
The stars linked
Resonating
And creating
The music of the spheres.

Dr. John R. Strum

What Do You Know About Me?

What do you know about me?
You can hear my words.
You can see the clumsy movements,
Limbs, not responding to commands.
Automatic messages
Undelivered.
I can hear the laughter of some impish God
Seeing me fall,
Seeing me making mistakes.
Simple things. Any child can do them,
But my poor body does not hear the message.
I am left lamenting
My stupidity.

What do you know about me?
Can you read my thoughts?
I so want to be strong,
A shelter in the storm.
I see the whiteness of my hair.
Where is the wisdom
So proudly proclaimed by my colouring?
I am frightened.
I am a snowman left out in the sun.
All you will have left,
Your only memories of me
Will be a stupid hat, a pipe, a carrot.
The aura of a melted smile.

~ *fini* ~

Made in the USA
Charleston, SC
15 June 2012